Around the World

Games

Margaret C. Hall

Heinemann Library
Chicago, Illinois

Customer Service 888-454-2279

Visit our website at www.heinemannlibrary.com

Designed by Lisa Buckley
Printed in Hong Kong

06 05 04 03 02
10 9 8 7 6 5 4 3 2 1

Library of Congress Cataloging-in-Publication Data
Hall, Margaret, 1947-
  Games / Margaret Hall.
    p. cm. -- (Around the world)
Includes bibliographical references (p.) and index.
Summary: Presents different kinds of games--including ball games,
running games, board games, and party games--and how they are played
around the world.
  ISBN 1-58810-476-1 (lib. bdg.)
  1. Games--Juvenile literature. [1. Games.] I. Title.
  GV1203 .H294 2002
  790.1--dc21
                    2001002470

Acknowledgments
The author and publishers are grateful to the following for permission to reproduce copyright material:

Cover photograph reproduced with permission of Bob Daemmrich—Stock, Boston Inc./PictureQuest

Title page, p.18 Momatiuk Eastcott/The Image Works; p.4 Tmongkol-Unep—Still Pictures/Peter Arnold,
Inc.; pp.5, 6 © Dinodia; p.7 Jeff Persons—Stock,Boston Inc./PictureQuest; p.8 Richard T. Nowitz/Corbis;
pp.9, 12, 15, 21 © Cathy Melloan; p.10 Keren Su/Corbis; p.11 Topham/The Image Works; p.13 Patrick
War/Corbis; p.14 © Victor Englebert; p.16 Jack Fields/Corbis; p.17 L. Goodsmith/The Image Works; p.19
B. Gibbs/TRIP; p.20 © Wolfgang Kaehler; p.22 Jacksonville Journal Courier/The Image Works; p.23
Deborah Harse/The Image Works; p.24 Still Pictures/Peter Arnold, Inc.; p.25 Sean Sprague/Panos Pictures;
p.26 Joe Viesti—The Viesti Collection; p.27 Haga Library Inc.; p.28 Paul A. Souders/Corbis; p.29 Lauren
Goodsmith/The Image Works

Every effort has been made to contact copyright holders of any material reproduced in this book.
Any omissions will be rectified in subsequent printings if notice is given to the publisher.

The author would like to thank her family—John, Alison, and Jason.

Some words are shown in bold, **like this.** You can find
out what they mean by looking in the glossary.

Contents

Games Around the World

Many children in Thailand enjoy jumping rope.

People all around the world like to play games. They play games inside and outside. They play with friends and by themselves.

This boy in India is playing a game called Snakes and Ladders.

Some games are only played in certain parts of the world. Others are played almost everywhere. A game might be a little bit different from country to country.

Playing by the Rules

Follow-the-leader is a popular game in India.

Most games have **rules** that players should follow. Some games do not have many rules. These games are easy to learn and easy to play.

A father and son in Japan play chess together.

Other games have many rules. It takes a long time to learn to play them. People often **practice** for years to become good at these games.

Playground Games

Four American girls are playing ring-around-the-rosie on their school playground.

Children everywhere play games like tag, ring-around-the-rosie, and hide-and-seek. These games have been played in the same way for hundreds of years.

These girls are playing blind man's bluff in Thailand.

Many playground games are the same no matter where they are played. The name of a game may change, but the **rules** are often alike.

Ball Games

A young girl in China plays ping-pong.

People play many games by throwing, rolling, kicking, and hitting balls. Balls can be made from wood, rubber, leather, plastic, or even paper.

These Algerian children are playing a ball game.

Pairs of people play ball games like catch or two-square. People also play ball games with groups of people split into **teams.**

Running and Chasing Games

Two girls in India play a chasing game.

Long ago, people ran to get places quickly or to escape from danger. They chased wild animals to use for food. Children played games to learn these **skills.**

These girls in England are having a potato sack race.

Children still play running and chasing games today. They have races of many different kinds. They also chase each other just for fun.

Games with Sticks and Stones

Children in Ghana enjoy a game of mancala. Their playing pieces are stones.

People often use **resources** found nearby as **playing pieces** for games. That is why games like **mancala** were first played with stones.

This type of mancala set is sold in stores. The playing pieces are made of plastic.

Games are still played with things found nearby. However, many games now use metal or plastic playing pieces instead of sticks and stones.

Jumping Games

These girls in Guatemala are playing hopscotch.

Jumping games are easy to set up and easy to play. The same game can often be played alone or with a group of friends.

16

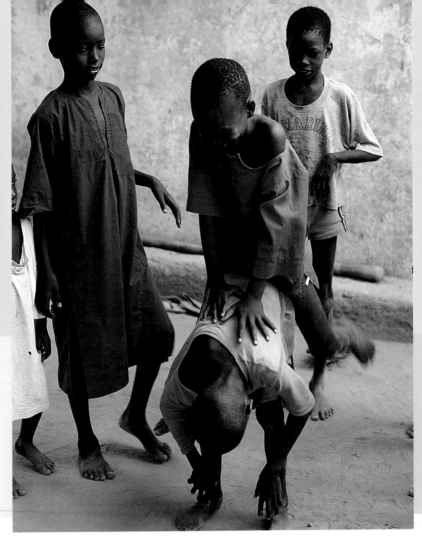

These boys in Mauritania are playing leapfrog.

Children play all kinds of jumping games. They jump over rocks and ropes. Sometimes they even jump over each other!

String and Rope Games

This Inuit girl in Canada plays a game called cat's cradle.

Many people play games with string. They may tell stories about their **culture** as they move the strings. The same stories have been told for hundreds of years.

Tug-of-war is a popular game in England.

Tug-of-war is a rope game that is played in many places. The winner is the **team** that pulls the hardest. Another popular rope game is called jump rope.

Marble Games

Children in Indonesia play a marble game.

Many children like to play marbles. Most marbles are glass. They also can be made from stone, metal, or clay. Some children play marbles with peas, beans, or nuts!

Marbles come in different sizes and colors.

Some marbles have special names. These names may be different in different parts of the world. Each kind of marble has its own use when playing a game.

Circle and Hoop Games

American children like to play a circle game called hot potato. The item used must be passed around the circle very quickly.

Some games are played in a circle. Often, players pass something around. Or one player runs outside the circle to catch another player.

Two Mongolian boys play a game by rolling rubber hoops.

In many parts of the world, children have fun rolling hoops over the ground. Sometimes they use sticks to push the hoops along.

Board Games

These boys in Malawi are playing a game called bao.

Some games are played on a surface called a **game board.** The board may be made from wood, paper, or stone. Often, the board is just drawn in the dirt.

24

Boys in Jamaica enjoy playing a game of checkers.

Many of the world's oldest games are
board games. The way some game boards
look today is much like when the games
were first played.

Party and Festival Games

Piñatas are a popular party game in Guatemala.

People play games because games are fun. They often play games when it is time to **celebrate** at a party or **festival.**

People in Thailand splash water on each other as part of Songkran. The water game is part of a religious festival.

Many festival games started as a way to teach people about their **culture.** These games often tell about the **religious beliefs** of the players.

More Games

This boy in Israel is spinning a top.

People play many kinds of games. They play with objects, numbers, and words. They run, skip, and jump. They throw, catch, and spin things.

A group in Mauritania enjoys playing a circle game.

All around the world, people have favorite games. They may play alone or with friends. But everyone plays for the same reason. They want to have fun.

Amazing Game Facts

✪ In Haiti, children play a game that is a lot like jacks. But instead of jacks, they use knucklebones from a goat! The game is called *osselets*.

✪ A game played thousands of years ago is still played today. It has many different names around the world. In Spain and Italy, it is called *dama*. In England, it is called *draughts*. In the United States, it is called *checkers*.

✪ The Chinese game of *mah jong* is like a card game, but it is played with tiles. The most beautiful tiles are made of hand-painted bones, ivory, or **bamboo.**

✪ The game called *go* is very hard to learn. Some Japanese people study the game most of their lives just to learn how to play it well!

Glossary

bamboo woody grass with a hollow stem

celebrate to have a party for a special event or holiday

culture belief system and ways of doing things among a certain group

festival time of celebration, usually with special events

game board surface with markings for playing a game

mancala board game played with stones or plastic pieces

playing piece something used to play a game

practice to do something over and over to get better at it

religious belief something a person believes about his or her god

resource something available for people to use

rule how something should be done or how people should act

skill something people need to know or be able to do

team group of people playing together, usually against another team

More Books to Read

Ajmera, Maya and John D. Ivanko. *Come Out and Play.* Watertown, Mass.: Charlesbridge, 2001.

Bernhard, Emery. *Time to Play: Children's Games Around the World.* New York: Dutton Children's Books, 1999.

Dunn, Opal. *Acka Backa Boo! Playground Games from Around the World.* New York: Henry Holt, 2000.

Lankford, Mary D. *Dominoes Around the World.* New York: Morrow, 1998.

Index